BEI BEI
GOES HOME
A PANDA STORY

CHERYL BARDOE

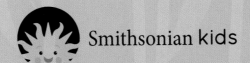 Smithsonian kids

 CANDLEWICK
ENTERTAINMENT

Keepers at the Smithsonian's National Zoo are excited.

It's August 2015, in Washington, DC, and they see a tiny shadow on an ultrasound image. This is the zoo's first glimpse of a fetus inside a giant panda mother's womb. The panda Mei Xiang, which sounds like "may-SHONG," is pregnant. But even with the ultrasound, zookeepers can't be sure when—or even if—she will give birth.

Three days later, an infant is born. Its squeals are very loud! For a species as rare as the giant panda, every new cub is cause for celebration.

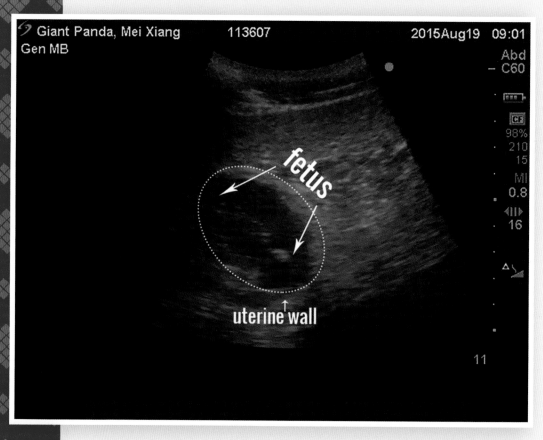

Just a few days before Mei Xiang gives birth, the shadow on this ultrasound picture shows a fetus that is about one and a half inches (four centimeters) long.

The first glimpses of the newborn cub come through the "panda cam" inside Mei Xiang's den. The mother puts her cub down for only a few minutes at a time.

PANDA FACTS

Giant panda pregnancies usually last from three to six months. The length varies because the fertilized egg can float freely for weeks inside the mother's womb until it attaches itself to the uterine wall and begins to develop. After mating, a female panda's hormones and behavior will suggest that she is pregnant—even if she is not. Plus, sometimes a fetus will stop developing and its cells will be absorbed into the panda mother's body. As a result, zookeepers often don't know if a panda is really pregnant until she starts to give birth! When a female spends hours in her nest, moving about restlessly, zookeepers watch closely to see if a cub actually arrives.

The two-week-old cub weighs one pound (half a kilogram). Mei Xiang and her cub spend a lot of time snuggling and snoozing.

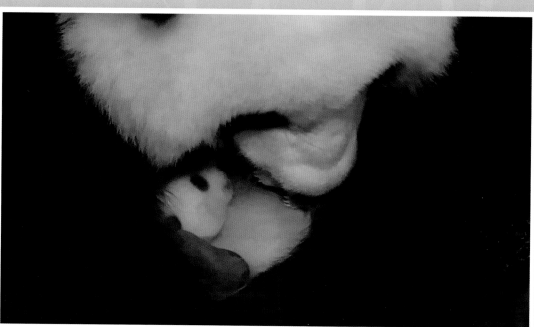

At first glance, the newborn cub looks more like a naked mole rat than a giant panda.

It weighs 5 1/3 ounces (151 grams). Mother Mei Xiang weighs 245 pounds (111 kilograms), which is more than seven hundred times larger. That would be like a human newborn having a mother the size of an elephant. Yet Mei Xiang's massive arms gently cradle her cub. She nurses her baby up to eight times a day and almost never puts it down.

PANDA FACTS

Mei Xiang births two cubs several hours apart. About half of giant panda births involve twins. The mothers, however, can produce enough milk for only one cub and quickly focus on the strongest twin. In other zoos, keepers have helped panda mothers rear twins by rotating the cubs every few hours—with one twin getting solo time with its mother while the other sibling is kept cozy and hand-fed by humans. Unfortunately, despite the zoo's efforts, Mei Xiang's weaker cub dies four days after birth.

The brand-new cub is completely helpless.

It cannot see or hear. This is why panda mothers remain in their dens for days after giving birth. Mei Xiang first steps out to eat some bamboo on day six, and when she does, zoo veterinarians step in. They listen to the cub's heart and lungs. They also take a sample of its DNA—it's a boy! By now, wispy white fur has sprouted and black markings are emerging around the cub's eyes, ears, and back. By three weeks old, the cub triples in size.

PANDA FACTS

In addition to zookeepers, a team of volunteers tracks the cub's progress around the clock through cameras in the panda den. Because giant pandas live alone, they are hard to study in the wild. At the zoo, observers record nursing, grooming, and communication. Information collected in these journals can help scientists protect pandas in the wild.

Here is the cub at three weeks old. Veterinarians work quickly to measure and weigh him in the moments when Mei Xiang briefly leaves her den.

This cub is an immediate celebrity.

In his first week, five hundred thousand users log on to the zoo's website for two million views inside the panda den. Fans also send notes and cards of congratulations.

Pandas in zoos are considered animal ambassadors from the People's Republic of China because that is the only country where they live in the wild. The first ladies of the United States and China, Michelle Obama and Peng Liyuan, host a ceremony in September to announce the new cub's name. He is called Bei Bei, which sounds like "bay bay," and means "precious treasure" in Mandarin Chinese.

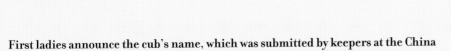
First ladies announce the cub's name, which was submitted by keepers at the China Conservation and Research Center for the Giant Panda in Wolong, China.

PANDA FACTS

In 1972, the president of China gifted a pair of pandas to the United States to honor closer ties between the two nations. Those pandas lived out their lives at the Smithsonian's National Zoo without producing any surviving cubs. Bei Bei's birth is the result of more than forty years of scientific collaboration between the United States and China around panda conservation.

Mei Xiang starts bringing Bei Bei out of the den at six weeks old.

He will remain inside the panda house, however, until he receives vaccines to protect him from common diseases.

With newly opened eyes, Bei Bei spends much of his awake time striving to work his muscles. He pushes his head up. He kicks his legs and scoots in circles. At three months—and a plump twelve pounds (nearly five and a half kilograms)—he takes his first wobbly steps on all four legs. A few days later, Bei Bei's ear canals open and zookeepers see him respond to sounds.

PANDA FACTS

Bei Bei is Mei Xiang's third cub. Her first cub, a boy, was born at the Smithsonian's National Zoo in 2005. Tai Shan, pronounced "tie-SHON," now lives in China as part of a research and breeding program. Mei Xiang's second cub, a girl, was born in 2013. Bao Bao, whose name rhymes with "wow," was weaned and living independently at the Smithsonian's National Zoo before Bei Bei was born.

By six weeks, Bei Bei's eyes start to open and tooth buds begin to develop inside his mouth. He can push up on his front paws and scoot around.

Bei Bei naps through a health check. He receives his first vaccination at about six weeks old. By five months, he will have completed the vaccinations needed to go outside.

Bei Bei becomes more active as he grows. He goes outside for his first snowfall. He climbs in the panda house. He also tries to climb out of the basket when veterinarians weigh him.

People love Bei Bei.

Nearly 7,500 people stream through the panda house on a single January day to see the public debut of this roly-poly, fluffy, puffy panda cub. Bei Bei puts his full personality on display: he is curious, social, energetic, and easygoing. Visitors delight in watching him climb rocks. They cheer when he bounces back up after falling down. They coo when he drifts off to sleep.

PANDA FACTS

At five months, Bei Bei weighs twenty-two pounds (ten kilograms) and still nurses twice a day. Pandas have special wrist bones that work like thumbs to allow them to pick up bamboo stalks as thin as a pencil, and Bei Bei uses his wrists to hold bamboo as he tries to chomp on it. At this age, however, the leaves mostly fall out of his mouth.

Sometimes Bei Bei is as interested in visitors as they are in him. While it may seem like he is posing for the camera, Bei Bei is just being his panda self.

At six months, Bei Bei goes outside to explore a world of new sights, sounds, and smells. He revels in the low branches of a tree. Giant panda cubs spend hours perched in trees—and out of harm's way—while their mothers eat. Bei Bei quickly discovers, however, that going up is easier than coming down. Fortunately, with flexible bodies and padding from thick fur, pandas are built to take a topple. Bei Bei also loves to climb on his mother . . . or tag her and dash away . . . or roll with her down a hill. Mei Xiang is a willing playmate for rough-and-tumble.

PANDA FACTS

Over time, Bei Bei catches sight of father Tian Tian, pronounced "t-YEN t-YEN," who enjoys a yard next to his. Bei Bei can also smell Tian Tian and nearby sister Bao Bao—a panda can detect another panda's scent from eighteen miles (twenty-nine kilometers) away. But these pandas do not bond. Adult giant pandas live alone, and fathers do not provide care for cubs.

The first time Bei Bei climbs a tree, he cries until Mei Xiang helps him inch his way back down. After that, the young cub gains confidence.

For his first birthday, Bei Bei has a Zhuazhou ceremony.

In this Chinese tradition, objects are placed before one-year-olds and whichever they touch first represents something about their future. For Bei Bei's party, the zoo hangs three posters on bamboo poles. In an unexpected turn of events, however, Mei Xiang is the first to investigate the posters. With Bei Bei trotting close behind, Mei Xiang reaches for one of the bamboo poles and ends up making the cub's choice for him. Bei Bei's symbol is the red Chinese knot, which represents luck and friendship.

Bei Bei also enjoys a giant birthday "cake" made of frozen fruit juice and decorated with apples, pears, sweet potatoes, and bamboo. Bei Bei now weighs seventy-three pounds (thirty-three kilograms), which is more than two hundred times larger than the day he was born. That would be like a human baby growing to be the size of a large polar bear in one year.

Three banners are displayed for Bei Bei's first birthday party. One banner shows bamboo, a symbol of good health and habitat. Another banner has peaches, a symbol of longevity. The third banner becomes Bei Bei's symbol.

Bei Bei and Mei Xiang are part of a conservation success story. While giant pandas are no longer endangered, we still must work to ensure their survival in the wild.

PANDA FACTS

September 2016 brings more reason to celebrate. The latest census of giant pandas counts more than 1,800 of these animals in the wild. This is nearly double the estimated number in the 1980s. Efforts to conserve pandas and the places where they live are making progress! As a result, giant pandas are now considered a vulnerable species instead of an endangered species. This change means that pandas are less in danger of becoming extinct, or dying out, in the wild.

RISK OF EXTINCTION

The International Union for Conservation of Nature evaluates the chances that a species—a kind of animal, plant, or other organism—may die out. These categories help to prioritize scientific research and conservation efforts.

CATEGORY	DEFINITION
Extinct	No living members exist.
Critically Endangered	A very high chance of becoming extinct within the next ten years, unless people take action.
Endangered	At risk of becoming extinct within the next twenty years, unless people take action.
Vulnerable	At risk of becoming extinct within the next one hundred years, unless people take action.

Bei Bei is a curious bear. Coaxing treats from feeders, gnawing on various textures and discovering different tastes, and climbing trees are ways he explores his world.

Bei Bei is a fast learner.

Each day he spends time training with zookeepers. First, he must learn his name so that he comes when called. Then he learns to touch a target with his nose, to stand up, and to present his paws. These behaviors will help keepers and veterinarians make sure Bei Bei stays healthy. Trainers cue each behavior with a hand signal and give Bei Bei lots of yummy rewards—sweet potatoes are his favorite.

PANDA FACTS

By Bei Bei's first birthday, his adult teeth have grown in, and he begins to actually eat bamboo. In November, keepers notice that Bei Bei stops eating and shows signs of being sick. Veterinarians discover that a lemon-size clump of undigested bamboo is blocking Bei Bei's system. They perform life-saving surgery, and Bei Bei makes a full recovery.

Having learned to be a successful panda, Bei Bei begins living separately from Mei Xiang at eighteen months. He is no longer a helpless cub and does not need his mother's milk. But he isn't quite an adult panda either and will continue to grow for several more years.

Bei Bei's diet is now mostly bamboo, along with fruits, vegetables, and special biscuits the zoo gives to leaf-eating animals. In the wild, bamboo is 99 percent of a giant panda's diet, and adults eat up to eighty pounds (thirty-six kilograms) daily. Munching and crunching and chewing and chomping can fill fourteen hours of the day. Pandas sit while eating. They use both front paws to shovel bamboo into their mouths, and their ears wiggle while they chew.

Bei Bei uses his powerful jaws, sharp front teeth, and broad molars to crush sturdy bamboo stalks.

Bei Bei always finds fun in his yard. He sometimes curls up to sleep with his red ball tucked in his arms.

Bei Bei is a playful panda with a flair for acrobatics.

He climbs trees and hangs upside down. He bends branches and slides—or crashes—to the ground. When a dusting of snow appears, Bei Bei dives in, rolls around, rubs it on his head, and celebrates with somersaults.

Keepers scatter toys and other items throughout Bei Bei's yard, so he may discover a large box to sit in, a red ball to chase, or an interesting smell. These things encourage him to use his natural behaviors, stay active, and exercise his mind. He especially likes to roll in the scent of pumpkin spice! Some puzzles have treats inside to reward Bei Bei's problem-solving skills. After a busy day, Bei Bei tucks himself into his hammock for a good night's sleep.

PANDA FACTS

With her youngest cub now independent, Mei Xiang shows interest in mating again. Hormones signal her interest to Tian Tian, even though they live in separate yards. Scent and sound are how pandas find each other to mate in the wild. Mei Xiang has a small window—about twenty-four to seventy-two hours—when she can become pregnant. Keepers watch both bears closely, since their behaviors will signal when it's the right time to put them together. And each year, panda fans hope for another cub to celebrate.

Bei Bei's thick fur may look soft, but it actually feels like a scratchy sweater. His fur grows in two layers: a coarse, long outercoat, and a finer, denser undercoat.

Bei Bei spends his final weeks at the zoo entertaining visitors and preparing for his journey. Keepers train him to walk through, and then to sit in, his travel crate. When the big day comes, Bei Bei is relaxed inside his crate as a forklift transports him to a truck that takes him to the airport.

Soon after his fourth birthday, Bei Bei travels to China.

Before he goes, visitors flock to say goodbye. Coming from across the country, zoo visitors write notes to Bei Bei, sample dumplings, and make friendship bracelets in honor of the panda who symbolizes luck and friendship.

Like the star he is, Bei Bei travels to China in a private plane. The 8,508-mile (13,692-kilometer) trip takes sixteen hours, which Bei Bei spends eating and resting in a large crate made of steel and plexiglass. Bei Bei is kept company by a zoo veterinarian and a leader from the giant panda care team who once held this now 240-pound (109-kilogram) panda less than twenty-four hours after he was born.

PANDA FACTS

Bei Bei travels on a cargo plane called the FedEx Panda Express, which is decorated with a giant panda decal. Bei Bei's older siblings traveled in the same way.

Bei Bei settles easily into his new home.

The Smithsonian's National Zoo team tells their Chinese colleagues about their new charge: Bei Bei loves to climb trees but doesn't like his feet touched. Sweet potatoes are his favorite, and he detests bananas. Bei Bei's training has always focused on hand signals, so he is not confused when his new keepers speak Chinese instead of English.

From the beginning, everyone has been preparing for this moment. Bei Bei's flexible, inquisitive personality helps him be comfortable with new experiences.

PANDA FACTS

Soon after Bei Bei arrives, he greets new fans. The public now visits him at a research center in Sichuan province that is dedicated to giant pandas.

In his new home, Bei Bei has an indoor enclosure with a hammock and an outside yard that is as large as he had at the zoo. Bei Bei's escorts also brought his red ball to his new home.

Perhaps one day, a descendent of Bei Bei will join pandas in the wild.

Bei Bei and his siblings are part of a worldwide effort to ensure that giant pandas always survive in their native mountains.

Where Bei Bei lives now is part of the China Conservation and Research Center for the Giant Panda. Researchers there hope to raise panda cubs who can succeed in the wild. Bei Bei cannot do this himself because he is too comfortable around humans. Keepers in China have begun donning panda costumes to help raise cubs who will be released into the wild. After Bei Bei is fully mature, around six or seven years, he may become the father to such a cub.

With a species as rare as the giant panda, that would be something to celebrate.

Bei Bei can look forward to a long, healthy life in his new home. Giant pandas tend to live fifteen to twenty years in the wild and about thirty years in human care.

⇒ GIANT PANDAS IN THE WILD ⇐

A skull found in southern China suggests that giant pandas have been around for at least two million years. The giant panda's native home, also called its habitat, is nestled in the mountain ranges of central China. Because temperatures are colder at the top of a mountain than at its base, pandas enjoy living at higher grounds during the summer season. Then they move lower during cold weather. Like the fur of other members of the bear family, a panda's thick, two-inch-long (five-centimeter-long) fur keeps it warm and dry even during winter. Pandas do not hibernate because their diet does not allow them to store up enough energy to last months without eating.

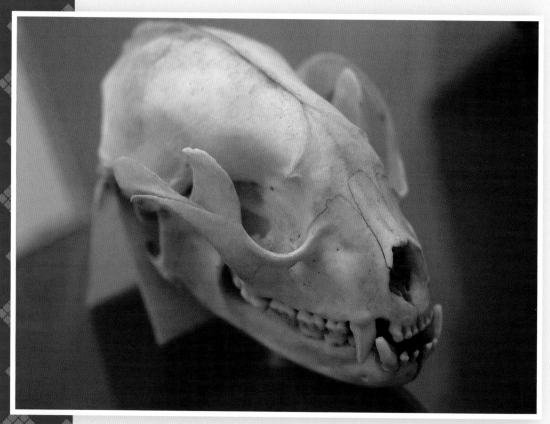

Bamboo is an ideal food because pandas can find dense thickets both high and low in the mountains of their range. Bamboo is not, however, packed with nutrients, which is why pandas spend so much time eating. Pandas eat bamboo stalks, shoots, and leaves. They strip off the tough outside of stalks to get to the softer inside. Unlike other plant eaters, pandas do not have specialized features—such as more than one stomach or specific gut bacteria—to help digest so much plant matter. Pandas need a lot of rest and sleep because their bodies spend so much energy accessing nutrients.

A giant panda's daily diet of tough bamboo causes a lot of wear and tear on its teeth. Scientists have discovered that the enamel on a panda's teeth can partially heal itself, which prevents small cracks from growing into big cracks.

⇒ WHY DO WE LOVE PANDAS ⇐ SO MUCH?

Pandas are the definition of cute, scientifically speaking. Mammal babies have several traits in common, including large eyes, chubby cheeks, big foreheads, and round bodies. These features trigger a chemical response inside the brains of all mammals—including humans—that makes us want to take care of them. This is why we find puppies, kittens, baby hedgehogs, elephant calves, and so many other young mammals irresistible. Giant pandas retain some of these features, along with a strong sense of playfulness, even as they grow into adults.

Giant pandas were first mentioned in Chinese literature two thousand years ago. Since then, they have become an important cultural symbol of China, representing peace and friendship. In modern times, they have also come to represent scientific collaboration and conservation.

Bei Bei demonstrates how giant pandas remain cute as they grow up.

⇒ HOW CAN WE HELP ⇐ GIANT PANDAS?

Giant pandas are considered "charismatic species," which means that they are a kind of animal that captures people's attention. For decades, giant pandas have inspired people to take action to help ensure their survival.

The giant panda's habitat is now a tiny portion of what it once was because of logging and the building of new roads and towns. Pandas need enough habitat to support each animal's solitary lifestyle and allow them to travel among territories to find food and mates. About two-thirds of giant pandas that live in the wild live in areas that China has designated as wilderness preserves.

We can help by supporting organizations that study pandas, that patrol habitats to prevent illegal logging, and that work with local residents to reduce impact on the panda's forests. In addition to other research, the Smithsonian's National Zoo and the Conservation Biology Institute are exploring ways to make it easier for wild pandas to travel between the different fragments of their habitat. Protecting wilderness for giant pandas also benefits the hundreds of lesser-known plant and animal species that live alongside them. Understanding the plight of giant pandas—and celebrating our progress with this animal—also inspires people to support conservation efforts that protect diverse plants and animals in other habitats.

PROCESSED POOP

n the lab, scientists dry and
rush panda poop before
nalyzing it.

his is what it looks like when
l the water has been remove

ARTIFICIAL
The Back-u

Observing pandas like Mei Xiang and Bei Bei in zoos helps scientists learn about giant panda biology and behaviors. This information can inform and focus efforts to save these animals in the wild. In addition to collaborating with the zoo, the Smithsonian Conservation Biology Institute conducts research at its headquarters in Front Royal, Virginia, and at field research stations around the world.

First US edition 2021

Library of Congress Catalog Card Number pending
ISBN 978-1-5362-1763-6

21 22 23 24 25 26 CCP 10 9 8 7 6 5 4 3 2 1

Printed in Shenzhen, Guangdong, China

This book was typeset in Filosofia.

Candlewick Entertainment
an imprint of
Candlewick Press
99 Dover Street
Somerville, Massachusetts 02144

www.candlewick.com